to walk in Paris

**Vignettes from two months
in the City of Light**

to walk in Paris

Vignettes from two months in the City of Light

SHARON BECKMAN & DAVID BECKMAN

McCaa Books • Santa Rosa

McCaa Books
1604 Deer Run
Santa Rosa, CA 95405-7535

First published in 2014 by McCaa Books, an imprint of McCaa Publications

ISBN 978-0-9960695-3-3

Printed in the United States of America
Set in Minion Pro
Cover design and photo by Sharon Beckman

www.mccaabooks.com

Table of Contents

Introduction

EACH MORNING at 7 a.m. we drank fruit, vegetable and *fromage blanc* smoothies in the tiny kitchen of our flat at 37 rue Descartes. Then we descended two flights to the street, which often smelled damp from the night's rain, and sometimes pungent of stale beer, from the late-hour student bar across the way.

We walked a half block north, turned right onto rue Clovis, skirted a last remnant of the 15th-century wall that once protected Paris, and angled down rue Monge, toward our health club for a workout. Back in the apartment we loaded a backpack with maps, guidebooks, sweaters, hats, an umbrella and a camera, and set out for some far-flung neighborhood to find lunch, preferably at a street-side café table. Then the real walking began. Logging four to seven miles on foot every day for two months tested our feet, legs, lungs and our French.

Which is exactly as we wanted it. For some time we'd yearned to know Paris close up and at a lingering pace. This time we wouldn't be tourists. We'd go local.

Writing vignettes was an afterthought. One day we just started, emailed them off and, encouraged by friends back home, continued. This book contains all eleven of them, plus a poem.

Our sojourn in Paris deepened our relationship with each other and enhanced our love affair with the city. To embrace the timeworn label City of Light is to revel in its profound beauty, but doesn't capture the hurly-burly, shoulder bumping, and traffic. Fortunately, years in New York had conditioned us for these.

Evenings sometimes brought the most memorable moments, when, after a salad, paté, baguette and glass of wine, we ventured out yet again, this time down rue Sainte-Geneviève and across the Place Maubert for an aesthetic, even spiritual, nightcap: moonlight touching Notre Dame's spire and sending the Seine sparkling, as if for the first time, westward under its bridges.

We hope we've captured impressions and sentiments worthy of Paris in our vignettes. And more importantly, that you enjoy them.

—Sharon and David Beckman

First Sunday

DB

T HANKS TO SHARON'S research, we had a plan for our first full Sunday in Paris—a trip to *Marché l'Aligre*, an outdoor food bazaar in a neighborhood of working people, shops, artists and artisans, reminiscent of Brooklyn before it became chic, or the Mission District in San Francisco before high-tech discovered it.

Our bus delivered us a block from the market, which occupies a large square and nearby streets, featuring Middle Eastern, North African and French merchants behind stalls of fruits, vegetables, cheeses, fish and meats. Vendors were intense, friendly and vocal, calling out their wares in singsong cadences. Soon the passageways between stalls were crammed with families, young couples, elderly people and tourists vying for elbow space. Our bag was soon heavy with dates, ham, cheeses, a cucumber, olives, and bread.

Needing a break, we found a nearby café and took a table at the curb for the quintessential Parisian snack: *croissants* and *café au lait*. Soon we were chatting with the young man at the adjacent table, an Irish expatriate furniture designer with an easy manner and Belfast lilt. He'd lived in Paris for 10 years, after stints in San Francisco and New York. He knew the neighborhood intimately, and gave us good advice for our walk.

Off we went, on to a trek along bustling streets with shops, cafés, and apartment houses. It turns out that the area has been vibrant for 300 years (hey, this is Europe). One house featured a plaque explaining that, in 1830, in the interior courtyard, a hot air balloon that had ascended on the other side of Paris had made an emergency landing.

By 4 p.m. the warm day was cooling, with fluffy soft clouds enhancing a blue sky. We took a bus back to the Left Bank. The city was suffused with a painter's light, so we headed to the Panthéon, passing Eric Kayser, considered to be among the very best bakeries. We pressed our noses against a window displaying seriously delectable-looking breads, tarts and cakes, then made our entrance, Euros at the ready.

On to the Panthéon, which was being extensively renovated and restored. Finished in 1790, it had been the tallest building in France until the taller Eiffel Tower reared its Erector Set head in 1889. A wide street, rue Sufflot, named for the Panthéon's architect, runs 300 yards from its front columns west toward the Luxemburg Gardens. Like a giraffe peeking over a tree on an African savannah, the Eiffel Tower, three miles distant, stands visible and aloof as if to say, "Take that, Panthéon."

It was the world's tallest structure until 1933, with the building, considerably further west, of our own Empire State Building. Which despite its height, is out of view from here.

Tired and satisfied with *un autre jour complet* we walked home by way of two tiny winding streets to a light dinner of paté, bread, cheese, olives, an avocado with a pool of vinaigrette in the space left by the pit, and the last of a bottle of Bordeaux left from the day before.

Oh, and a pistachio and apricot tart from Eric Kayser.

Fashion

DB

TODAY WE HAD LUNCH on boulevard Saint-Germain, which Sharon and I particularly like, one reason being that it reminds us of upper Broadway in our old New York neighborhood. Sitting at our café, watching the sun-splattered street and the passing people, we ordered beer and salads. After a bit, Sharon nudged me and said, "Look at the woman over your left shoulder."

She was a middle-aged Parisienne a few tables back. "Her hair," Sharon said. Moderately curly, salt and pepper, asymmetrically cut, perhaps three inches long, with a slightly up and forward bias. The effect was casual, subtle and fetching.

"Toni Wilkes would look good with her hair that way," Sharon said. (Sharon, it turns out, had recommended her Healdsburg hairdresser to Toni – a good friend back home.)

Our lunch arrived and we lost ourselves in eating, drinking and doing what everyone here does—watching the passing street scene, not just for its color and flair, but as a plein air lesson in human possibility, intention and what it is to present the self, unguarded or otherwise, to others.

As we finished lunch, Sharon said that at one point she'd looked up and that the woman had caught her eye and they'd both smiled. Sharon had pointed to her own hair and had made the universal thumb-to-fore-finger, "I approve" sign. The woman, in turn, had done the same thing, complimenting Sharon on <u>her</u> hair.

Ah, fashion—one of its pleasures is that two strangers who have an innate gift for it find each other and naturally, sweetly, gesture mutual admiration.

Ego

DB

ONE HOT AFTERNOON we headed toward the Luxemburg Gardens, passing St. Sulpice, a church built in 1646, and the large square in front of it, featuring chestnut trees and a fountain.

We sat on a bench, finding an oasis in the shade and sound of falling water. The fountain is imposing—70 feet tall, with three levels where water splashes down to form pools. At the corners of the second level four huge stone lions protect large statues of four bishops at the level above. All was peaceful, as children played near the benches, and people found relief from the heat under the trees. Other than everyone's modern attire, and all the traffic sounds, it could have been any century among the last who-knows-how-many.

A few benches from us a thin, shirtless young man in red shorts stood and walked toward the fountain. As he climbed awkwardly six feet up to the first level, he gestured back to a friend with a camera. Shin-deep in water, he then turned toward us, raised his arms and gave a guttural cheer like a football player after a touchdown—"Yeeeaaaah!" Next, he climbed onto the back of one of the lions, stood off balance, then half jumped, half shimmied to the second basin and raised his arms. His chest was concave, his body hair black and straight. "Yeeeaaaah. I did it."

He was American.

Fifteen feet up now, he walked back and forth, kicking water, grinning. An odd silence pervaded the square as people watched him. He contemplated ascending to the next level, to join the bishops, but instead approached the edge to look six feet back down at the lion's back.

"Now what?" he said to no one and everyone. He sat on the basin's lip, looking suddenly small, and extended a bare foot toward the lion's back. "Wow," he announced, " I didn't think how I'd get down."

I realized what, besides his behavior, I didn't like about him: his assumption that everyone must be fascinated by his plight.

As he floundered in indecision, I thought I sensed what others in the square were thinking: we earn what we get, and character is destiny. The man sat again, measured distance and risk, and finally half fell, half slid onto the lion's back and from there to the basin below. Arms out, face exultant he screamed, "Yeeeeeaaaah, I did it!" He posed for good measure then jumped to the ground and, face flushed, padded back to his friends.

Not to further mar our walk, I resisted a confrontation in which I itched to tell him what an embarrassment he was, and instead fell into rumination on nationality, public behavior and mores. Then a thought came that overarched these and pleased me more: regardless of his nation of origin, he was demonstrating a human truth worth remembering.

Exiting the square I said to Sharon, "An ego is a terrible thing to waste."

Music and Serendipity
SB

THIS PARTICULAR SUNDAY, like most of ours in Paris, started with a trip to a market—this one just west of Place de la Bastille, allowing us to photograph the neighborhood nearby where my friend, Kristine, is renting next year.

After accomplishing our picture taking, we walked to the market, which was more extensive than we imagined. The markets are such a treat in Paris, with stall after stall of the most beautiful displays of fruits, vegetables, meats, fish and specialty food imaginable.

After an hour we headed for Place des Vosges in the Marais, a magical square surrounded by its impressive symmetry of matched brick houses with slate roofs and dormer windows over arcades filled with art galleries and restaurants. Before entering we heard uplifting music wafting through the entrance to the arcade. A harpist had set up on the sidewalk and was playing as if in his private concert hall. Further on, we encountered a French quartet playing swing music. I felt like dancing through the arcades like Juliette Binoche and Willem Defoe in "The English Patient".

We timed our departure to get to a theater to see "Rush," an American movie about the intense rivalry of two Formula-One auto racers 30 years ago. The considerate ticket seller told us that the film was in French, not English with subtitles as we had assumed (how on earth did he perceive that we weren't French?). So, not wishing to test our command of the language, we went into *flanneur* mode, and followed our noses, with our attention being drawn upward by an interesting rooftop here, or spire there.

I noticed a group of buildings that looked like artists' ateliers set into old arches. They turned out to be just that, set into the spaces created by an overhead viaduct that once supported a railroad line. As we walked by the mostly empty stores, we passed a furniture store and saw a sign for a concert that was to start there in two hours. The owner, a fashionable middle-aged woman with a warm smile, came out and invited us to return for what she guaranteed would be an outstanding performance by two accomplished musicians—a pianist and cellist.

Since we had time, she suggested we walk the three-mile green belt on the railroad bed directly above. It proved reminiscent of the enchanting and popular Highline in downtown New York. I had wanted to see both the *Viaduc des Arts* and the *Promenade Plantée*, so it was sheer luck that we wandered into these two sites.

But the real piece de resistance was the concert itself. We were seated in the most elegant folding chairs, the store being Yamakado, which manufactures very upscale furniture, mostly in leather. These chairs cost $1000 apiece (for <u>folding</u> chairs, for God's sake!). The piano was a Steinweg, the German founder of Steinway—the name he adopted when he immigrated to the U.S. We were treated to Beethoven's Sonata for Cello and Piano No. 3, and a Brahms sonata. The sound was very pure in that cave of stone with vaulted ceilings. I was reminded how, in Beethoven's time, women swooned when they heard his music (did you see the movie "Immortal Beloved"?). I did a little swooning myself and we walked out on a cloud of uplifted spirits from our good luck wandering into this extraordinary experience—pure serendipity!

To Your Health

DB

The sky so pale and trees so slender
Seem to smile at our small distresses.

—Paul Verlaine

THIRTY-NINE RUE DESCARTES, the building next to ours, exudes character. On the ground floor is a very good restaurant—La Maison de Verlaine, whose owners, Brigitte and Nicolas, and headwaiter, Stathis, became favorites of ours. Tall, outgoing, ever attentive, Stathis was setting up tables every morning, and unfailingly greeted Sharon and me as we embarked on our Paris adventures. And, as rue Descartes leads to rue Mouffetard, one of the oldest and most food-intense streets in Paris, with twenty restaurants and a five-day-a-week, open-air food market, La Maison de Verlaine marks an entry to a demi-paradise, and Stathis is its gatekeeper.

The restaurant's name derives from Symbolist poet Paul Verlaine, who lived in the building until his death in 1899. Coincidentally, Ernest Hemingway rented the top-floor room as a writing space from 1920–25. They each merit a plaque near the door. But whose spirit dominates—the poet of sensory images and *fin de siecle* yearning, or the novelist of pared-down sentences and riveting modernist prose? A few weeks ago we gave it to Verlaine.

The day started in a class at our health club. Sharon and I were on side-by-side mats doing arm rotations when I felt a small "kerthump" on the right side of my neck. My right inner ear replied: "kachung." Immediately, the room left its axis, lifting itself from bottom right to top left, then rotated and revolved at the same time, like a space capsule going rogue. I closed my eyes.

When I reopened them the room was doing ballet spins and I was clammy and nauseous. I tried to stand. Silvio, our trainer, said, "*Continuez, monsieur David, continuez!*"

Certain I'd had a seizure or stroke, I did the only reasonable thing—went into full denial and announced with forced calm, "Just a touch dizzy. Nothing…"

Silvio, not understanding, said, *Faites comme votre femme…comme votre femme.* ("Do like your wife!")

I saw Sharon executing the exercise moves in her usual robust and accomplished way. Resisting shouting "Goodbye world!" I sat quietly and watched the room do the jitterbug.

Half an hour later Sharon and I walked home hand in hand. I was buoyed by the fact that I was alive, probably stroke-free (I could speak clearly, knew my name, President Obama's, my Social Security number and could count to ten in two languages). What's more, the world had stopped spinning and had reduced its threat to resume each time I moved my head.

I emailed Dr. Joseph at Santa Rosa Kaiser to describe my symptoms. He replied that the culprit was vertigo and advised Dramamine. Sharon went out for the meds and I lay down. The room was somewhat steady but my head felt like a hot air balloon readying for liftoff. After taking the Dramamine and napping, I felt better and suggested we walk to the Luxemburg Gardens.

"Then lunch?" Sharon asked.

Any thought of food made me nauseous. "For you but not me."

It was a sunny day with a fresh breeze, and the park looked, as it so often does, like a paradise invaded by all manner of mortals, most bearing the smiles of those who have found, well—paradise. We chose a bistro on a busy corner across the street from one of its tall, wrought iron gates. Before ordering I went down a winding staircase to the restroom. That's right—a <u>winding</u> staircase. I found myself in a small corridor that was having, of all things, a private earthquake.

In the restroom I realized I was hallucinating. Everything appeared bizarrely small, including the urinal, sink and paper towel dispenser. I mean doll's-house tiny. My world had gone Alice-in-Wonderland.

I exited, seeing that there were two more doors, one with an "H" etched in the glass, for *Hommes*, the other with an "F", for *Femmes*. That first room? It had an "E", for *Enfants*. Children. Obviously <u>small</u> children. The joke was on me but I didn't risk laughing.

Back home, I emailed Dr. Joseph, reporting mild improvement. He replied: "Keep taking the Dramamine, get rest and you'll be back enjoying the City of (spinning) Lights." Such a comedian.

I also emailed my alternative healer, Deborah Myers, whose Jin Shin Jyutsu work has, over the years, soothed my bad back and assorted aches and pains. She replied with some spot-on energy balancing tips that I immediately put to use.

The next morning I sat up too abruptly, a move that the room disliked. It tilted and re-tilted like a boat in a chop. Sharon was sure that I needed food, and had a brainstorm. "We'll order in." And she disappeared out the door.

I slept fitfully, dreamt of barrels going over Niagara Falls, then heard doors open and close, and the next thing I knew, who stood before me but Stathis! Smiling, he bent over me. "So sorry you are not feeling well, David. I hope a good lunch will help." He patted my shoulder and gave me a hug. Then he was gone.

I stumbled into the living room to see that Sharon had two place settings on our table. Shrimp and avocado on a bed of fresh spinach for her and for me, *Salade Perigourdine*—greens, duck, paté, olives, walnuts, with a baguette on the side.

My head cleared and my stomach saluted. Miracle! My appetite came roaring back. I ate everything.

The next day it was as if the vertigo had never happened. *Merci*, Sharon. *Merci*, Dr. Joseph. *Merci*, Deborah. *Merci*, Stathis. *A votre santé!*

Pharmacie/Droguerie/Stathis

SB

Yesterday, David developed a case of vertigo in our exercise class and had to take it easy, limiting us to an afternoon outing and an early dinner. (See his previous vignette, *To Your Health*.) This morning he woke up with a worse case, and I realized I needed to spring into action. No fear, I would consult my pharmacist.

Earlier in our trip I had a cough that kept me up at night. My friend, Kristine, who had lived in France, encouraged me to consult with a pharmacist because they do much more diagnosis and prescribing than in the U.S. So, I had referred to my trusty i-Pad translation app and developed my "script." After the required *Bonjour Monsieur* greeting, I'd faced a serious and attentive man and had recited my highly studied inquiry. He'd nodded and pulled out a box of lozenges and a bottle of cough syrup. Later, when my cough persisted at night, I'd once again explained my dilemma, and he had recommended another nighttime syrup. It had worked wonderfully, so he had taken on God-like qualities for me.

I referred to him as *my* pharmacist.

For his vertigo, David had emailed his Kaiser doctor and gotten a recommendation for Dramamine. Armed with a new script, I set off for my pharmacy. Kristine was so right about pharmacies doing more here. While I was waiting for *my* pharmacist, another was attending a workman who had obviously hurt himself on a job. She applied spray and bandages right in the aisle. Once again, after I described symptoms, the pharmacist gave me his knowing nod. He went down to the basement and returned with a product for *mal des transport*, which should either help David's vertigo or deal with his commuting problems!

The other man in Paris whom I have become dependent on is the one at the *droguerie* on the corner. My favorite bedtime reading here is Barrie Kerper's "Paris: The Collected Traveler." It has a wonderful essay on a *quincaillerie* which is a hardware store, and a *droguerie*, an all-purpose store densely stacked with merchandise hung floor to ceiling with products only the owner could find. Not to worry if you don't see the product you're looking for because the inventory extends to the cellar, accessed through the trap door.

My droguerier provided me with a sponge, a window cleaner, a lock, an extension cord, an adapter—there was no request he couldn't fulfill in spite of my limited French.

Kerper's book makes the comparison of her local *droguerie* with large department stores, where the service doesn't compare. She ends with, "I happily pay more to preserve this intensely human and agreeable experience of my daily life. Call it the price of civilization."

I end this vignette with Stathis, the friendly Greek waiter from the restaurant next door who greets us every day as we leave our apartment. I realized that we should take advantage of living next to a restaurant by having the chef prepare a meal I could bring back to the apartment. When I took my basket down to get it, Stathis insisted on bringing everything up to our apartment, and giving David a "get well" hug! Can you believe our luck—having an apartment next to a restaurant where the waiter makes house calls?

Chiaroscuro

DB

ONE SUNDAY, SHIFTING shades of light and dark accompanied us through Paris. Embarking on a market outing well north of the Seine, we sought out *Marché des Enfants Rouges* (Market of the Red Children). Its name derives from an orphanage that once stood on the site, where the children wore red uniforms.

The sun was out, and as fluffy clouds filtered the light, Paris presented, street by street, a face alternately bright and dark.

On the bus ride, Sharon and I talked about the day's breaking news—the U.S. might at any moment send missiles into Damascus, with full support of the French. That we were a now a continent and ocean nearer to Syria made the prospect feel more immediate. That we were reading about it in the *International Herald Tribune*, and seeing reports on French television, made it oddly remote. But however it's reported, the question was the same: time to kill again as national policy, and in our names?

We found the market in a large interior courtyard, with stalls of fresh fish, poultry, cheese, bread, pastries, olives, couscous, and meats—this in a neighborhood already crowded with shops offering a bounty of the same. Indeed, just walking from the bus stop involved traversing a gauntlet of food.

Have you ever experienced "Stendhal's Disease"—the loss of breath, energy and even consciousness upon spending too much time in a museum? The author Stendhal suffered this dark side of esthetic hunger in Florence in 1817, leading to a breakdown. So the disorder has been named for him.

Sensing that the affliction could strike in a French market, though the cause be piles of goat cheese, pyramids of fresh fruit, stacks of pastries, fish displayed in crushed ice and baskets of sausages, rather than Old Master paintings and sculpture, we were *en garde*.

We trolled the market bravely and until weak, then exited to a sunlit café facing the green, peaceful Square de Temple for hot chocolate, croissants and orange juice. This square, now a sun-dappled leafy play space for strollers and children, was once a fortified residence for medieval Knights Templers, among the fiercest fighters of the Crusades, containing a palace, church, walls and drawbridge. During the Revolution, Louis XVI and Marie Antoinette were held here as revolutionaries planned their execution. For them, any sunlight may have had no effect on their royal dread.

Contemplating how long-past European political upheaval and violence seem so remote in the U.S., and even from Paris' bucolic present, we gathered ourselves and headed back into the market, scoring a round of St. Vincent Burgundy cheese, a block of smoked salmon, fresh ginger and tomatoes.

Next we ventured through tiny winding streets of the Marais, the ancient Jewish section, now known more for trendy boutiques and restaurants. Having gotten into the habit of reading plaques on buildings signifying artists, writers or scientists who worked or died on the premises, we spotted one on the aged wooden façade of a narrow three-story synagogue. The plaque—gleaming white stone with handsome carved letters—said, in French, that in this building, in 1944, three young men and their mother were tortured to death by German Nazis.

We were stunned to silence that such cruelty had happened just feet from where we stood. But we were also moved that such shame is now so publicly recorded. Just down the street, another plaque marked a spot where many French children were shipped to concentration camps from occupied Paris.

However, few things being just what they seem, we've since come to learn that French sympathizers aided the occupying Germans in atrocities and displacements, and that the campaign to mark where Nazis committed dire acts was in part to make sure the focus is solidly on them, not the collaborators.

Back at the Seine, Notre Dame's bells rang out. Sharon had found a small food/wine/beer festival on a riverside *quai*, so we descended stone steps to join a boisterous crowd for lunch of sandwiches and risotto.

Waving to tourist boats going by, we tapped our feet to a brass band playing 1960's hits, and looked up at Notre Dame's towers, spire and flying buttresses cutting high into a blue sky as late-day shadows lengthened to the east.

Chiaroscuro, indeed.

Confession

SB

A T LUNCH TODAY David and I had something our weight-control regimen has long ago banned—a hamburger. To be absolutely accurate, I ordered the *crabe roumalade* and David, with heavy encouragement from me, chose the hamburger. After watching me sample my lunch rather indifferently, he asked if I would like to trade. Never have you seen plates move across a table so quickly. I dove into the hamburger.

What was so special about it? Besides the perfect pinkness, caramelized onions, and an ooze of melted blue cheese, what made it irresistible was its familiarity. Not that it was a particularly Parisian hamburger, with unique ingredients only available within a mile of the Seine, or that it was wrapped in bread baked in special French ovens that produce such memorable baguettes. No, just an ordinary bun around a good old American-style hamburger. This ecstasy was in spite of the fact that I've been turning my nose up at any café in Paris that caters to Americans by advertising hamburgers. I've tended to be attracted to those cafés and brasseries that have *Salade Complete à la Marine*, with salmon and clams, or *Salade Perogordine*, with smoked duck, paté and gizzards!

Later in the day I convinced David that the only way we were going to get any takeout soup for our dinners at home was to go to Picard's, a frozen food emporium. The first time I passed one, with it's low counters and super-white interior, I assumed it was an electronics store. The fact is, Picard's is very popular with the French: there are over 250 of them in France, offering everything from *soupe* to *noix*. We're talking very high-level frozen food!

In we went, approaching each freezer suspiciously, thinking, "I can't believe we're in Paris and we're buying frozen food!" We, who make such a point of going to the markets every Sunday to bask in the glory of the great displays of fresh fruits, vegetables, meats, fish and cheese!

Okay, we decided that we would just try the soup—after all, it would go well with the salads that we make faithfully each night in our apartment after pigging out at lunch. Somehow, by the time we got to the checkout, a package of Chicken Cordon Bleu had appeared in our basket.

Heading home, we passed the Panthéon, Eglise St-Étienne-du-Mont and Lycée Henry IV—all Parisian landmarks embodying France's history, pride and, in the case of the Lycée, a school where, for generations, France's future leaders have been groomed.

But our illusion of acquired sophistication was shot as we skulked home with neither fresh bread, paté, cheese nor pastry. Instead, a bag full of frozen food! As we passed stylish Parisians on the sidewalk, we knew that their backward glances marked us as just two more doltish Americans.

We got home and heated up our purchases. They were delicious. One of the books on Paris that I'm reading has surmised that even well-known chefs who are pressed for time, sneak into Picard's on their way home, quickly sculpt a tomato rose and voila—dinner.

Tomorrow, I swear it's back to Paris eating at its best and freshest.

Les Martiniquaise
DB

ONE SUNDAY, SHARON and I headed to northeastern Paris for another market—*La Chapelle*. The district has a robust ethnic mix with African, Indian, Pakistani, Southeast Asian and Caribbean people, shops, music, styles and food.

We found the permanent market pavilion of brick and glass where vendors specialize in traditional Parisian cheeses, charcuterie, bread, produce and fish. But there were two larger stalls, essentially restaurants without walls; one Martiniquais, one Moroccan. The first, overseen by two women, was heavy with spiced aroma of fish and chicken in various sauces and curries. Across the brick floor a Moroccan cook and two assistants tended ceramic platters of lamb, beef and chicken tajine simmering with olives, onions and orange slices. Both had tidy tables set up for customers.

Sharon and I engaged the Martiniquaise women—one stout, smiling, round-faced and with an easy manner, the other taller, elegant, with an ascetic face and rimless eyeglasses. We said that we had honeymooned in their country 33 years earlier, at the Hotel Beauregard. They both showed pleasure at this news.

Sharon ordered chicken curry, but I stepped across for Moroccan tajine with couscous and vegetables. We chose a table on the Moroccan side, and a friendly competition followed in which each server tried to outdo the other in efficiency and friendliness. It was a tie in all respects, with us the winners.

Upon finishing, we returned to the Martiniquaise and I said that I admired their national poet Amé Cesaire, whom I'd been studying. The first said, *Mais oui, Il est merveilleux.* ("Yes, he's wonderful.") Then she asked if I'd read Rafael Confiant; I hadn't.

The tall woman stepped up and I immediately sensed a seriousness of purpose. She said, *Alors monsieur, il y avait Franz Fanon.* ("Then, sir, there was Franz Fanon.")

I knew Fanon's work, particularly *The Wretched of the Earth*, unofficial required reading when I was in college, and among the most influential anti-colonial books ever written.

Oui, I said, *Il était plus fort.* ("Yes, he was very powerful.")

She fixed me with an intense gaze, and said, *Il était le meilleur de tout.* ("He was the best of all.")

I held her eyes and nodded, suddenly aware of my whiteness and of engaging a Caribbean woman about a book laying bare the toxicity in so much white colonial behavior of the past centuries. The kind we Americans are hardly innocent of in Vietnam, Iraq and elsewhere—call it what we want.

Do these women really have poetry, pride and love of freedom near the core of their lives? Or am I romanticizing them? Very probably the latter.

The tall one eyed me a moment longer, as if to read my mind, then extended a slender hand, which I took in mine.

"Bon chance, Monsieur," she said.

I replied, *"Bon chance Madame, et merci."* But before I could turn away the first woman said, in English, "But monsieur, I love Amé Cesaire so much. In fact, I named my daughter Amy in his honor. So you see...."

I saw.

Mysteries
DB

WHEN JULIUS CAESAR came, saw and conquered a small fishing village on the Seine in 52 A.D., the Romans had themselves an agreeable northern outpost, making them the first Paris-loving foreigners. They laid out streets, built elaborate baths and an arena that still exist, and a forum, which doesn't. What I like about this are the unknowns—how did Paris look and feel then? How did Romans get around—on foot, by cart or horse? Bus? Metro? If on foot…what was their footwear? Sandals? Boots? Birkenstocks?

It's a mystery.

I bring this up because on a recent walk in the Marais we passed a trendy shoe store into which Sharon disappeared while I loitered outside watching other strollers' urban gaits and rhythm while the sun illuminated the pale stone and wrought iron balconies of apartment houses. These, while being 150 years old or more, nevertheless postdate Roman times by 1,400 years. What was here in the interim?

More mystery.

After some moments Sharon reappeared from the store. "Come see," she said.

Back inside, she pointed to a pair of black ankle-high boots with two wide straps that said "biker" and "hip woman" at the same time.

"Really nice," I said.

"Think so?"

The owner approached: a 30ish, sleek, black-clad woman with an open face, green eyes and—well, a fine Roman nose. She wore a sheer low-cut sweater revealing a tattoo of the word VIDI centered below her collarbones in a two-inch-high flowing script with a sinuous vine climbing halfway up the V.

She said, in accented English, "I am glad you return. The boots, Madame, have your name all over them."

Sharon said, "Still, I'm not quite sure." Then to me, "Ready for lunch?" We excused ourselves and went to a bistro around the corner where Sharon confessed that she liked the boots, but hunger had overtaken her (a not uncommon occurrence), clouding her judgment.

I said, "Those boots are you." She paused over her *moules-frites*, and I detected a decision behind her eyes.

When we re-entered the store a half hour later, the woman awaited us as if by agreement. Pointing to the boots and said, "Madame, they are you." My exact words.

As Sharon tried the boots on, a pair of men's shoes grabbed my attention. High-tops with brown leather at heel and toe, red suede amidships overlaid with

41

three angled strips of patterned brown fabric, and leather medallions framing the number 62.

I liked them, especially as they featured prominently the year I graduated from high school. The woman approached and said, "Monsieur, there's a mirror in back."

My face probably showed my thought: for what?

Sharon said, "To see how they look on you from the side and back, of course."

"No need," I said.

Sharon and the woman exchanged a conspiratorial look. Sharon said, "Unlike women, men don't need to look at shoes from more than one angle."

The woman rolled her eyes, and reverted to French: *Oui, les hommes! Ils sont si faciles.* ("Men! They're so easy.")

Afterward, Sharon explained to me that women tend to look at shoes from the viewpoint of others. What impression will they make? Whereas a man focuses on comfort, and how they look to him alone. *Vive la différence!*

We made our purchases, and on paying I couldn't resist an obvious question, and feeling brave, posed it in French: *Votre tattoo, Madame, qu'est-ce qu'il signifie?* ("Your tattoo, Madame, what does it mean?")

Il est un de trios mots, mais vous ne pouvez pas voir les autres deux. ("It's one of three words but you can't see the other two.")

"Ah," I said. "Of course—Veni, Vidi, Vici. I came, I saw, I conquered. Julius Caesar."

"Exactly, that's me."

I awaited an explanation and not getting one, asked, "Really? How so?"

She gave me a sly look. "Easy. Julius Caesar—I am just like him." She boxed our shoes and placed them in a cloth carrying bag. "Goodbye, monsieur et madame, and happy walking."

We said goodbye, stepped to the street, waved back to her and headed lazily through a crowd toward rue Saint-Michel, the modern incarnation of the earliest Roman road in Paris, and walked up the hill toward our neighborhood. Skirting the Luxemburg Gardens, one-time site of the Roman forum, we ruminated on just how a shoe storeowner might be like a Roman emperor. But to no avail.

In Paris mysteries are everywhere.

Cubism and Life after Paris

SB

Toward the end of our stay, David and I saw a Georges Braque retrospective at the Grand Palais. Braque is most associated with Cubism, and along with Picasso taught us to look at a form not only from the front, but to explode the planes and see something in its totality at the same time. He made the point that his art met you at the surface of the canvas, took your eye in different directions and planes, eventually meeting back at the surface of the canvas where the art exists. I decided that I wanted to leave that exhibit with some new ideas about my life and not just file away images and move on.

I thought about how often we look at objects and people without inquiring about what's happening on their various planes. Do we take comfort in what's familiar, fearing that too much examination might lead to disappointment and confusion? Do our preconceptions about people give us comfort because we don't have to spend energy on spinning out their infinite possibilities?

Take for example a man on the Metro today. David and I were headed for the 16th Arrondisement to walk a new neighborhood. A rather sad, disheveled man ambled up the aisle. "Oh no" I thought, "another person interrupting the quiet of our outing with a plea for money. Because he doesn't have a job? Or he needs Euros for his sick mother?"

He stopped in front of us. "Here it comes...why us? Because he knows we're tourists?"

He said, *"Excusez moi, Monsieur, votre écharpe est par terre,"* pointing to David's scarf, which had fallen on the floor. He smiled a smile that radiated kindness.

Haven't all those years working in prison taught me to get beyond appearances? Why do I jump to conclusions about people before I get a chance to explore their many dimensions? I'm stuck on the image that I see first—the violin before Braque reveals its other side, and the music beyond. Now I want to explore those other facets, notes and planes and meet back at the surface of the canvas, which is the person in front of me.

When I left home for Paris, my friend Carmen said to me, "I have this feeling that Paris is going to change you." And now it has. Braque has opened my mind to the Cubist experience, letting me explore life from newer and richer perspectives.

Merci, Georges!

45

Paris
DB

light   cathedral towers straining west   gardens
      where trees wear scarves and
people plant themselves deep
putting out roots and leaves that
fall   come fall   streets matrix at corners
     buses troll   daring history

in the metro below rue Monge an old man
     in tattered sweater
birdwalks toward us to say   *monsieur, votre*
     écharpe est par terre
("sir, your scarf is on the floor.") then bends
     to retrieve it for
me   we resist all history here   all
light for fear it has more to say than we
     and feels it more
and will far past when these words wash
     away toward
Argenteuil

we can't get enough of your river   as if finer
    life were flowing here
and we tourist-lemmings head for it day
and night looking for some truth awash
near Pont Neuf since 1607 when writers
    sharpened quills   dreaming
under scudding clouds that beauty was
    only here   and
art

beauty is here and art and forgotten hands
    that strained to be a part of it   at
the tip of Ile de la Cité   randy Henri IV
established
a pubic bone of land where he dallied long
and named a narrow cobbled triangle
    opposite   the female essence of Paris
we walk there now   thirsty
    for meaning and a glass of red
Bordeaux

Acknowledgments

Our thanks to Sonoma County's online review, *Counter Culture Magazine*, and its editor, Chip McAuley, for featuring the following vignettes during 2014: "Fashion," "Ego," "Chiaroscuro," "Mysteries," and "Cubism and Life after Paris."

Also thanks to Waights Taylor Jr., of McCaa Books, for his patience and good counsel in shepherding our vignettes into book form.